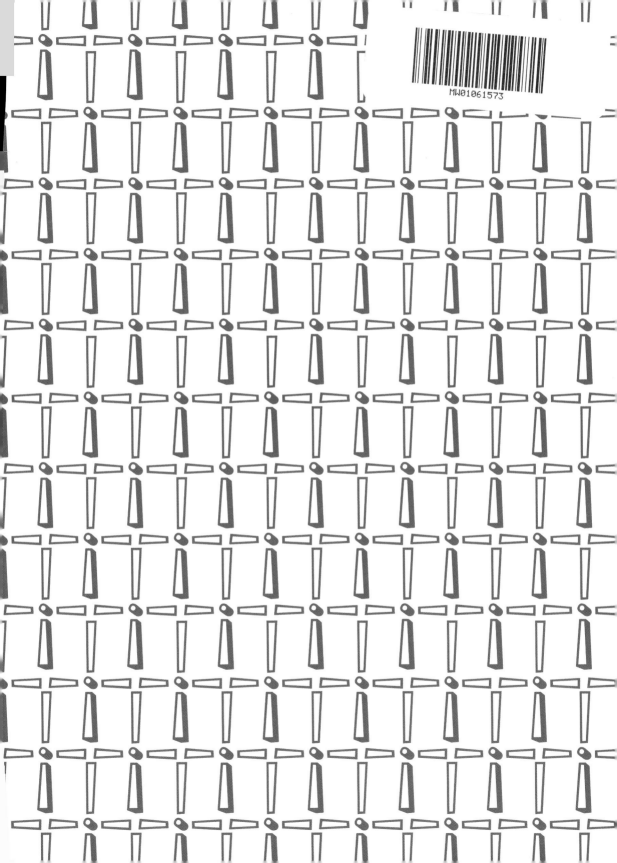

Noah's Ark
AND OTHER BIBLE STORIES

BY REBECCA GLASER
ILLUSTRATED BY BILL FERENC AND EMMA TRITHART

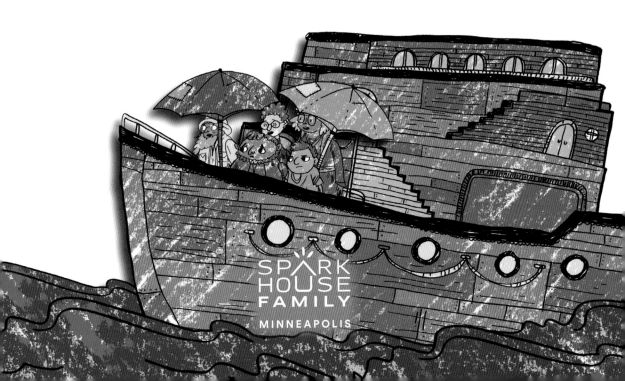

SPARK
HOUSE
FAMILY
MINNEAPOLIS

Contents

24 23 22 21 20 19 18 17 16 15   1 2 3 4 5 6 7 8
ISBN: 978-1-4514-9994-0

Book design by Toolbox Studios, Dave Wheeler, Alisha Lofgren, and Janelle Markgren
Illustrations by Bill Ferenc and Emma Trithart

Library of Congress Cataloging-in-Publication Data

Glaser, Rebecca Stromstad, author.
  Noah's ark and other Bible stories / by Rebecca Glaser ; illustrated by Bill Ferenc and Emma Trithart.
      pages cm. — (Holy moly Bible storybooks)
  Summary: "An illustrated retelling of the story of Noah's Ark and other common Bible stories" — Provided by publisher.
  Audience: Ages 5–8.
  Audience: K to grade 3.
  ISBN 978-1-4514-9994-0 (alk. paper)
1. Noah's ark—Juvenile literature. 2. Bible stories, English—Old Testament. I. Ferenc, Bill, illustrator. II. Trithart, Emma, illustrator. III. Title.
  BS658.G53 2015
  222.109209505—dc23
                                2015011203
Printed on acid-free paper

Printed in U.S.A.

V63474; 9781451499940; AUG2015

Creation

In the beginning, there was nothing, until God created the heavens and the earth. "Let there be light!" God commanded. And light sparkled across the water. God named light day and darkness night.

At the end of Day 1, God admired creation and said, "It is good."

On Day 2, God placed a bright blue sky high above the water.

Color in the sky.

Splish, splash! Dry land popped up from the water on Day 3. Green plants, tall trees, and colorful flowers burst from the earth.

4

God made the big, bright sun to shine during the day and the round, pale moon to shine at night. Stars twinkled all across the night sky on Day 4.

On Day 5, the water in the seas bubbled and gurgled and filled with fish. High in the sky, birds chirped and squawked and soared through the air.

Creeping and crawling, hopping and running, animals of every kind filled the earth on Day 6. Lions roared. Cats meowed. Horses neighed.

"Now," said God, "I will make people in my image." God created a man and a woman. God blessed them and put them in charge of caring for all of creation.

After six days of hustle and toil,
God took one day to rest.
God blessed Day 7 and made it holy.

With a smile and a laugh,
God looked over all of creation
and said, "It is very good!"

Adam and Eve

The first people God created were named Adam and Eve. They lived in the garden of Eden, where they had everything they needed. God had just one rule:

"You may eat fruit from any tree, except this one in the middle of the garden."

One grim day a serpent slithered up to Eve.

"Thisss tree has the sssweetest fruitsss!" the serpent hissed. "Try sssome."

"But God says no!" Eve replied. "If we eat that fruit, we will die!"

"You won't die," the serpent said. "Eat the fruit from this tree in the middle of the garden. Then you'll know what'sss good and what'sss evil. You'll be like God!"

Count the fruit on the tree.

Eve picked a fruit from the tree. **CRUNCH!** She took a juicy bite, then passed the fruit to Adam. **CHOMP!** Adam chewed and swallowed.

Gasp! Adam and Eve realized they were naked! They covered their bodies with leaves and hid.

"Where are you?" God called. Adam jumped up and blamed Eve. Eve leapt out and blamed the serpent. They hung their heads in shame.

God punished the serpent and Adam and Eve for breaking the one rule. After creating clothes for Adam and Eve, God sent them out of the perfect garden into the world. God would be with them there too.

Noah

God's creation grew and grew. But the people forgot about God. They fought with each other and destroyed things. They worshipped beings other than God.

In the entire world, only one man remembered God. His name was Noah. God said to Noah:

"I am going to flood the whole earth. Everything will be washed away. Build a giant boat— an ark! Fill it with two of every living animal."

"Do everything I have told you, and I will save you and your family."

Noah obeyed God. He sawed wood and hammered nails. Board by board, Noah built the ark.

Two at a time, animals waddled, stomped, and crawled onto the ark. When all the animals were aboard the ark, Noah and his family went inside.

Kerplunk, drip, splash! The rain began to fall.

Draw other animals that might have been on the ark.

It rained, and poured, and rained some more. The water rose higher and higher. The ark rocked back and forth. Everyone inside stayed dry.

After forty days, the rain stopped. Noah sent a dove to search for dry land.

When all the earth was dry,
God placed a rainbow in the sky.

"I will never flood the whole earth again,"
God promised. "This rainbow is a reminder
of my promise!"

Abraham

Abraham and his wife, Sarah, were faithful to God, but they were worried. Even though God had promised them a baby, they didn't have one. They were old—old enough to be grandparents or even great-grandparents. When would God's promise come true?

One night, God spoke to Abraham: "Don't worry. You will have a son. Count all the stars in the sky. That's how many grandchildren and great-grandchildren and great-great-grandchildren you will have. Your family will continue to grow and grow."

How many stars do you count?

Abraham and Sarah would have to wait many more years for their baby, but they trusted in God's promise.

Sarah and Abraham

One blazing hot afternoon, God sent three men to visit Abraham. When Abraham spotted them, he jumped up. "Hurry!" he called to Sarah. "Make bread for our guests!" Abraham rushed to prepare some meat.

Fill the sky with pictures of food you like to share with guests.

Abraham served the visitors, then sat down with them. **Splash!** The visitors washed their feet. **Slurp!** They drank the milk. **Chomp!** They ate the fresh meat.
"Where is your wife, Sarah?" the men asked.
"Soon she will have a son!"

Sarah was listening by the tent. "Ha-ha-ha!" she laughed. "I am old. Abraham is old. We're too old to have a baby!"

But God keeps promises. Soon Sarah was expecting a child. When the baby was born, Abraham and Sarah named him Isaac.

Rebekah and Isaac

When Abraham and Sarah's son, Isaac, grew up, Abraham knew it was time for Isaac to get married.

Abraham went to his chief servant. "Go to my homeland," Abraham said. "Find a wife for my son Isaac."

The servant took the camels and traveled a long way to find Abraham's people.

After a long journey to Abraham's homeland, the servant stopped by a well and prayed. "God, help me find a wife for Isaac. If a woman offers a drink of water to me AND to my camels, let her be the one."

Just then, a woman named Rebekah came to the well. She offered water to Abraham's servant AND to his camels! The servant knew Rebekah would become Isaac's wife.

The servant asked Rebekah and her family if she would marry Isaac. They said YES! Rebekah traveled back with Abraham's servant.

Soon Isaac and Rebekah got married, and God blessed them.

More Activities

LOOK AND FIND

Find the numbers in the Creation story on pages 3-8.

God created for 6 days and rested on Day 7.

Find the

in the Adam and Eve story on pages 9-12.

God's punishment for the serpent was to make him move on his belly instead of legs.

Find the

in the Noah story on pages 13-18.

A dove is often used to stand for peace.

Find the

in the Abraham and Sarah story on pages 23-26.

Sarah laughed when she heard she would have a baby. The name Isaac means "laughter."

Find the

in the Rebekah and Isaac story on pages 27-30.

Wells were popular meeting places for people in Bible times.

ACTION PRAYER

Creator God,

Thanks to you for what is dear. *(touch fingers to chin and lower hands to say "Thank you" in sign language)*

We'll take turns, shout out our cheer *(cup hands by mouth like a megaphone)*

For things we love, on Earth right here. *(point down toward the ground)*

I love _____ . *(act out or make the sound of each person's idea)*

Jump for joy. Shout hooray! *(jump up high)*

Bless us each and every day! *(hold up one finger on each syllable for seven total)*

Amen!

MATCHING GAME

Match the person from the Bible with the fact about them.

1. I was 600 years old when the flood began.

2. My name means "princess."

3. My name means "laughter."

4. I am the first woman God created.

5. I offered water to visitors, including camels!

6. I am the first man God created.

7. My name means "father of many nations."

1. Noah; 2. Sarah; 3. Isaac; 4. Eve; 5. Rebekah; 6. Adam; 7. Abraham